KT-225-912

Design and Make
CLOTHES
AND SHOES

Helen Greathead

FRANKLIN WATTS
LONDON · SYDNEY

Contents

Why do we wear clothes?

People wear clothes for all sorts of reasons: to keep cool or warm or to protect their skin from the sun, rain and wind. Shoes, hats and gloves protect feet, heads and hands, too. But clothes are not just practical — they have become part of the way people express themselves, their cultures and their personalities.

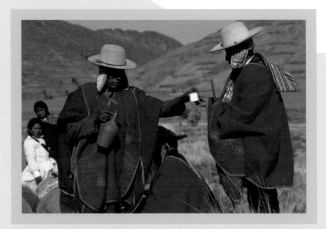

Simple but stylish

Clothes don't need to be complicated to make. In South America, the poncho is really just a blanket with a hole in it to slip over your head. In South-East Asia many people wear simple sarongs.

Talking kimono

In Japan, kimono can serve different purposes. Kimono actually means, 'things to wear' and at one time, people in Japan had a different kimono for every occasion. Your kimono said something about you, such as how old you were or whether you were married.

What do your clothes say?

These days, we can dress more or less how we please. Our clothes often show what sort of person we are. Choose from the projects in this book and see if you can make your outfits say something about you.

4

A few hints and tips

Here are a few other ideas to help you get started.

Finding materials

• Ask your family and friends, look in second-hand shops and scrap shops (see page 31).
• Buy small quantities of material – look in the remnants box in your local market, haberdashery or fabric shop.
• Always clear plenty of space to work. Fabrics are best cut on a smooth, hard surface. The floor is as good as anywhere!

Pattern making

• Use newspaper to make patterns. Stick pieces together with masking tape. Use greaseproof paper as an alternative.
• To make a pattern that is symmetrical, fold the paper in half and draw one half of the shape you need and cut it out across the fold through both layers of paper.
• Always allow at least 1 cm for a seam, unless the instructions say otherwise.
• Once you've made your pattern, pin it onto the fabric and then cut around it.

Hemming

• Where you have cut out material, you will need to hem the edges to stop it fraying. You can either hem using a simple running stitch (see page 7) or use an instant hemming fix. You can buy this from haberdashery shops and simply iron it on. Always get an adult to help you when ironing.

Be prepared

Here is a collection of things you will need to make the clothes and shoes in this book. You can collect things gradually and store them in a large box.

Getting it right

• To make sure you make your clothes and shoes the right size, it's a good idea to make a mock-up first using scrap pieces of material.
• When you are ready to make your actual item, tack the material together with running stitch before you sew it. Use colourful thread to make it easier to remove the tacking afterwards.

Things to collect

Scissors

Different thicknesses and colours of embroidery thread, cotton and wool

Pins, bodkins and different sizes of needle

Newspaper/ greaseproof paper

Tailor's chalk

Thimble

Tape measure   Hemming fix

Sewing machine and an iron and ironing board. Always get an adult to help you use these

Old bucket or bowl (ask before using!)

Plenty of salt

Cold dyes

Rubber gloves and apron or old shirt

Fabric paint and pens

Fabrics: old sheets, quilt covers, blankets, pyjamas, curtains, clothes, scraps of material, fake fur, fake leather, felt, chamois leather, any interesting textured fabrics

Old cereal boxes and packaging

SEA SALT

SULTANA BRAN

6

PVA glue

Double-sided tape, masking tape; gaffer tape

Interesting scraps of lace, rikrak, and other trimmings

Elastic bands

Ribbon

Sequins

Leather thonging

Pompoms

Beads

Buttons

Stitches

We use different stitches for different reasons. Here are three important ones. Always start off by tying a knot in the end of your thread.

Running stitch

Push the needle through the fabric and back out again to make a neat row of stitches that look the same on both sides. Use small running stitches for hemming, too. Use a larger version of running stitch to tack things loosely together so that you can try them on for size.

Overstitching

Overstitching is ideal for joining two raw edges of material together. Holding the edges together, push the needle up from the bottom and pass over the edge and up through the material again.

Blanket stitch

Blanket stitch is useful for neatening raw edges (see page 21). Working in from the edge of the garment, push the needle through and up to the edge. Wind the thread round the needle. Pull the needle through and push it in again.

A simple sarong

A sarong is easy to make, and it's stylish, too.

Challenge
How many different ways could you wear a sarong?

Look at this!

A sarong is a piece of fabric that wraps around your body. These days, everyone is wearing them! The pattern gives the sarong its style.

✱ How do you think the sarong is tied?

✱ Why are sarongs practical?

Design and select

Make a tie-dye sarong for yourself. Think about the pattern you want to create and the colour you will use. Which fabric will you choose? We cut up an old, white cotton sheet and used elastic bands and cold dye, with plenty of salt, to colour it.

Make

1 Cut out a rectangle of fabric as wide as your outstretched arms, that reaches from your armpits down past your knees. Hem the top and bottom edges only (see page 5).

2 Make sure your fabric
is completely clean,
then wet it thoroughly.
Hold the fabric up from the
centre and tie elastic bands
all the way down, leaving
10 cm between each one.

Challenge
How can you create a
different tie-dye pattern?

3 You should wear an apron or old shirt and
rubber gloves when you're using dye.
Carefully follow the instructions enclosed with
your dye to colour the fabric — get an adult to
help you. When coloured, put the dyed
fabric in a plastic bag and tie it up.
Leave it somewhere warm for two hours.
This will make your pattern stronger.

Challenge
How could you dye
your sarong two
different colours?

4 Take out your sarong and remove the elastic bands.
Open it out and hang it up somewhere to dry. When
dry, snip the sides to make them look like tassels and admire
your design! How will you wear your new sarong?

9

Customise a T-shirt

You don't always have to make new clothes from scratch. Decorating a plain T-shirt is easy and it looks great, too!

Design and select

Use a plain T-shirt to make a girl's decorated top. What will you use to decorate it? Draw a sketch of your ideas. Cut out samples of fabric. We used scraps of patterned fabric, broderie anglaise and sequins.

Challenge
How would you customise a boy's T-shirt?

Make

1 Most plain T-shirts have a high neckline. If yours does, use tailor's chalk to draw round the edge of a plate to make a lower neckline. Draw the neckline higher at the back. Carefully cut along your chalk line.

Challenge
Turn a plain T-shirt into a crop-top.

2 Try the T-shirt on inside out. If it is too long, mark the length you want with chalk. Take the T-shirt off and mark a straight line all the way round. Cut off along the line and hem carefully.

3 Tack some broderie anglaise onto the neckline and around the bottom of the T-shirt. Sew in place with two neat lines of running stitch (see page 7).

4 Cut out shapes from different fabrics and arrange them on your T-shirt. Ask for help to use an iron to fix them on with hemming fix, or sew them on with one of the stitches on page 7.

Challenge
How would you customise a pair of jeans?

5 Sew on any other decorations you want, like sequins or buttons. Finish off each sleeve by sewing on a fabric band and show off your T-shirt design!

11

Fisherman's trousers

These simple, groovy trousers are worn by fishermen in Thailand!

Design and select

Make a pair of colourful trousers without complicated fastenings – you can just tie a knot in the top of these to hold them up! Draw some sketches of your ideas. How long will they be? What fabric will you use? We've used a sheet from a second-hand shop.

Make

1 Sit across the fold of a large sheet of folded newspaper with your legs apart, as shown. Draw small dashes around your inside leg to your ankle, then your outside leg to just up past your waist. Get a friend to help if you can't reach that far!

2 Draw a solid line 2 cm around the outside edge of the dashed line to give enough room for a seam. Cut out your pattern. Unfold the paper and use it to cut out two trouser shapes in your chosen fabric.

Challenge
How could you add a belt?

Challenge
How could you make your trousers baggier?

A

B

3 Measure the pattern across the top and along the outside leg.

A

B

4 Cut out two rectangles in your fabric to these measurements.

5 Making sure you keep the patterned sides together, tack and then sew the pieces like this:

Seams

6 Tack and then sew the outer edges together and around the inside leg. Snip into the curve (see page 15). Hem the top and bottom of the trousers. Now turn them the right way out and try them on. Tie, wrap or roll them down to fit!

Challenge
Adapt this pattern to make a pair of drawstring trousers, or some dungarees!

Fun fur hat

A fun fur hat will really warm you up in the winter.

Design and select

Make a fun fur hat for yourself. Look at different types of material you could use and draw some designs. We used leopard-print fake fur!

Challenge
What other fabrics would keep you warm?

Look at this!

In some parts of the world, people wear real fur to keep warm. This man lives in Tibet where temperatures fall well below 0°C.

* What sort of fur do you think his hat is made from?

* What do you think it feels like?

Make

1 Wrap a tape measure round your head, across the tops of your ears. Push two fingers inside the tape measure so that your hat will not be too tight. Read the length of the tape and add 3 cm extra to this measurement to allow for the seams.

Challenge
How could you give your hat a rim?

2 Use tailor's chalk and a ruler to mark two strips of fur, each half the width of your measurement and about 22 cm high.

3 With the material right-sides together, tack the sides to make a tube. Try on the hat to check it is big enough. Sew up the sides.

4 Flatten out the hat, so that the seams are in the middle, and draw a curve shape across the hat with the tailor's chalk. Tack along the line and try on again to check for size.

5 When your hat is the right size, sew along the curve and remove the tacking stitches. Trim off any excess material. Carefully snip into the fur on the curve, as shown below. Turn your hat the right way out and pop it on!

Challenge
How could you add earflaps to keep your ears warm, too?

Challenge
How could you make a summer hat with a peak?

Bouncy flip-flops

Make some flip-flops to put a spring in your step!

Design and select

Make a pair of flip-flops using everyday materials. Sketch out some ideas and stick on fabric scraps to find the best combinations. We used dress fabric and leather thonging. The sole is made from bubblewrap and thick card.

Challenge
How could you decorate plain, readymade flip-flops?

Look at this!

People wear flip-flops all over the world. They are ideal for wearing in hot countries.

✱ Why do you think they are so popular?

✱ What materials are used to make them?

Make

1 Draw round your right foot on a piece of card, add 5 mm extra all the way round. This is the template for your flip-flop. Use it to cut out six layers of bubblewrap and two pieces of card.

2 Stick the six layers of bubblewrap together with PVA glue and then sandwich them between the top and bottom layers of card, as shown.

3 Cut out a piece of fabric using the template, adding 4 cm extra all the way round. Turn the template over and cut out a second piece of fabric, exactly the same size as the template, for the sole.

4 Cut two small disks of fake leather and make a hole in the middle of each with a sharp pencil.

5 Place your foot on top of the cardboard and bubblewrap sandwich and mark between your big toe and second toe. Use your mark as a guide to make a hole all the way through with a pencil. Make a hole in the same place on the larger piece of fabric, too.

6 Loop a piece of leather thong and thread the loop through the bubblewrap sandwich. Push one fake leather disk over the loop at the top and one over the ends at the bottom. Glue both disks down in place on the cardboard.

7 Push the thong through the hole in the large piece of fabric cut in step 3, leaving a 2–3 cm loop. Trim the ends of the thong on the bottom of the flip-flop and stick down.

8 Fold the material down and stick it to the bottom of the flip-flop, cutting small slits as you go to make this easier.

9 Push a folded piece of dress fabric through the leather thong loop and place your foot on the flip-flop. Pull the fabric tight and tuck under the sole. Glue down the ends.

10 Make sure everything is stuck down flat and neatly on the sole, then glue the smaller piece of fabric you cut out in step 3 to the bottom to finish it off. Decorate the edge of the flip-flop with rikrak. Repeat these steps with your left foot to make the second flip-flop.

Baby slippers

Make some soft, comfy slippers for a baby you know.

Design and select

Make and decorate a pair of soft moccasins suitable for a baby. Draw some basic slipper shapes and stick on fabrics and accessories to try out ideas. We used fake leather material and pompoms. You could use felt instead.

Look at this!

These moccasins are really comfortable to wear.

✳ What material do you think they are made from?

Make

1 Draw round the baby's foot on a sheet of paper to make the pattern. Draw another line around the foot shape, adding 1 cm for the seam. Round off the toe to make the shape symmetrical.

Seam allowance →

2 Cut out a shape like the one below. Measure the baby's instep – line A. Make line B as long as B on the baby's foot. Add a 1 cm seam all the way round.

1 cm seam allowance →

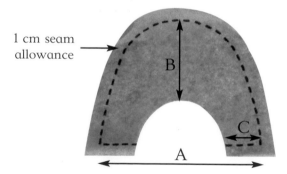

Challenge
Use this method to make slippers for yourself!

18

3 Use masking tape to gently stick your pattern to the fake leather and cut out carefully.

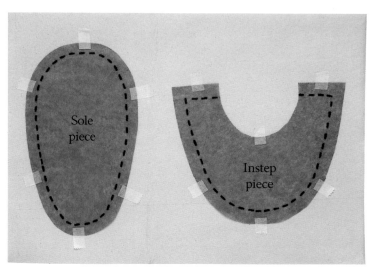

Sole piece

Instep piece

4 Use embroidery thread to sew the instep to the sole by overstitching (see page 7). Measure around the baby's heel (D) and line C (see page 18) and draw a rectangle as shown, right, adding a 1 cm seam. Cut out carefully.

D

Heel piece

C

Seam allowance

5 Sew the heel piece to the sole. Stitch up the sides to join the heel and instep. Turn the right way out.

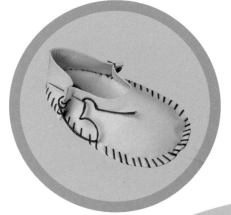

6 Decorate the front of the slippers with pieces of your material, snip the sides to make a fringe. Sew on some pompoms and the extra material with bright thread. Cut out an extra strip of material to go round the heel and stitch on. Ask the baby to try her new slippers.

Challenge
Decorate the slippers to look like a flower or a lion's face.

A cosy poncho

A poncho is really simple to make. It's easy and fun to wear, too!

Design and select

Design a poncho from warm, woven fabric. Find pictures of ponchos, traditional and modern, and make up a collage of your ideas. What fabric will you use? Will you add any decorations? We cut up an old blanket!

Look at this!

This man lives in Bolivia, South America. His poncho slips over his head to keep his upper body warm.

✱ How do you think this poncho was made?

✱ Why is it so practical?

Make

1 Hold your arms out to the side and ask for help to measure from one wrist to the other. Use this measurement to mark two diagonal lines on your material and join up the edges to make the square. Cut out your material. Make a mark in the centre.

Challenge
How could you knit your own poncho?

←25cm→

2 Fold the blanket in half diagonally. Draw a line 25 cm long that cuts through the middle of your central mark along the fold. This is the hole for your head.

3 Use blanket stitch (see page 7) in a matching colour wool to finish off the neckline.

(see page 7)

Challenge
Could you add a collar or hood?

4 Measure 6 cm in from the edge of the blanket and draw a line all the way around with tailor's chalk. Stitch along the line. Now cut up to the stitched line with scissors to make the tassels. Slip on the poncho and give it a twirl!

Challenge
How else could you make tassels or add on decorations like beads?

Furry moonboots

These boots won't protect you from snow, but they make great slippers!

Design and select

Make a fun pair of moon boots. Draw boot shapes on paper and stick on different textured fabrics. Which do you like best? We used spotty fake fur, thick foam and card. Follow the steps below using scrap materials before you make the finished boots.

Look at this!

All over the world people have designed amazing boots for harsh winter weather.

✱ What do you think the boots are made from?

✱ How are they decorated?

Make

1 Stand on a piece of cardboard, draw around your foot and cut out. Cut out a piece of foam the same size. Put your foot on the foam and make the heel and toe shapes shown below by wrapping strips of cardboard around your foot. Stick another piece of card over the end of the toe and stick down with masking tape.

A is from the top of your foot to the side of your heel

D

A

C   B

2 Cut out your fabric for the boot following the pattern shown, adding a 1 cm seam. Use the measurements from the inner shoe you made. Decide the leg height of your boots – line E.

1 cm seam

side   back   side

E   toe   E   toe

A   A

B   C   D   C   B

22

3 Sew the side pieces together along edge E with right-sides together, as shown.

Challenge
Could you use two or more fabrics?

4 Stitch the back piece (D) to the side pieces you just sewed (above), with right-sides together, to form a tube. Sew the two toe pieces together along the curved edge and then attach to the tube along the edge A (right).

5 Cut out a sole using your inner shoe as a template. Stitch the sole to the rest of the boot with right-sides together. Hem the top of the boot. Turn the right way out.

6 Cut another sole out of fake leather and stick it onto the sole. Repeat all these steps to make the other boot. Put the cardboard inner shoes in and your boots are ready!

Challenge
How could you decorate the boots?

23

A dressing gown

Make a summer dressing gown that's like a Japanese kimono!

Design and select

Design a summer kimono with a simple belt. Draw kimono outlines. What fabric will you choose? Will you add any decorations? We used an old quilt cover and pillow cases.

Look at this!

In Japan, women's kimonos are made from beautiful printed silks. Men's summer kimonos are much simpler and made from cotton.

✱ What shapes make up the kimono?

✱ How do you think they are fastened?

Make

1 To make the pattern for your kimono, work out the following measurements: elbow to elbow(A); shoulder to knee (B); shoulder to elbow (C).

2 Draw a rectangle on a large sheet of newspaper. The length is measurement B and the width is A. Add 1 cm all the way round for the seam and cut out. Pin onto your fabric and cut out carefully. Make a slit at each shoulder for the arm hole, this is length C, as shown (right).

Challenge
Print on a Japanese symbol with fabric paint.

A

C — Cuts for armholes — C

Side panel | Back panel | Side panel

B

← Fold here →

1 cm seam allowance

24

3 Fold the side panels onto the back panel so that the seams line up. Tack and then sew together at the shoulders, leaving about 5 cm unstitched near the neck. Make sure the material is right-sides together.

C

1 cm seam allowance

2xC

4 Cut out your sleeves from one of the old pillow cases. Use line C for the width and twice that for the length; add an extra 1 cm for the seams. Hem the outside length of each sleeve. Fold each sleeve in half, right-sides together, and sew up the top seam.

5 Lay the kimono out with the sleeves in place. (Gown and sleeves should be inside out.) Tack and then sew the top of each sleeve into the kimono, as shown.

6 Hem the rest of the sleeves and across the neck, front pieces and bottom.

Challenge
Make a dressing gown with long sleeves.

7 To make the belt, measure around your waist and cut out a long strip of material twice this length and about 40 cm wide. Stitch right sides together to make a tube, leaving one end open. Turn right way out and overstitch the end.

Pirates ahoy!

Most children love playing pirates. Why not create a pirate outfit for a little brother or sister – or for yourself!

Design and select

Design a complete pirate costume from things you can find at home. Find some pictures of pirates and sketch out your idea. Which fabrics will you use? We chose blue felt, gold buttons and braid for the waistcoat, a sheet for the trousers and rayon for the belt and scarf.

Make

Challenge

How could you make a pirate hat?

Waistcoat

T-shirt shape

Waistcoat outline

1 Fold a T-shirt in half and place it on two folded sheets of newspaper, as shown. Draw around the T-shirt.

2 Adapt your T-shirt shape to make a waistcoat outline, adding on 1 cm extra for the seam. Draw an L-shaped armhole, square off the neck and raise the bottom edge.

3 Unfold the newspaper and cut out the patterns. Pin one pattern to a large piece of felt for the back.

4 Fold the second piece in half again and cut a diagonal line to make the V-neckline, as shown below. Cut the pattern in two at the fold. Pin to the felt and cut out all three pieces.

5 Tack and then sew together at the shoulders and sides. Ask for help to flatten the seams with an iron. Turn your waistcoat the right way out. Sew on buttons, and braid around the edges of the waistcoat.

Trousers

1 Lay a pair of trousers folded in half on a folded sheet of newspaper with the front of the trousers along the fold. Use the shape of the trousers to draw your pattern. Add a few centimetres extra at the sides to make your pirate trousers a bit baggier.

2 Now draw your pirate trousers shape, adding 2 cm for the seam. Mark the length you want them to be.

3 Cut out the newspaper shape, unfold it and use to cut out two pieces in your trouser material.

4 Cut zig-zag shapes across the bottom of the trousers and snip again at the top of the cut like this to stop the material fraying (left).

5 Place the two trouser pieces right-sides together and stitch along the curved edge, as shown (right). Ask an adult to help you iron the seams flat.

Sew →

← Sew

6 Fold your trousers so that the seams are now in the middle. Sew up the remaining edge along the crotch, as shown (right). Trim away any extra fabric and cut into the curved seam (see page 15).

Sew → ← Sew

7 Fold the waistband edge down 2–3 cm and get an adult to help you iron this flat. Sew along this seam to make a tube for the elastic. Leave an opening of about 5 cm to thread the elastic through.

8 Cut a piece of medium elastic long enough to go round your waist, with 10 cm extra. Use a safety pin to thread the elastic through the waistband. Pin the other end to the trousers as you're doing this so it doesn't get lost.

9 When the elastic is through, pin the two ends together. Turn the trousers the right way out and try on to work out how tight the elastic needs to be. Cut and stitch the elastic together. Sew up the waistband.

Challenge

Could you make a toy sword or dagger for your pirate?

Belt

Cut a strip of fabric long enough to wrap twice round your pirate's waist. Fold the fabric in half along the length, right-sides together. Sew along the edge, cut zig-zag ends and turn the right way out.

Headscarf

Cut a triangle of fabric. Make sure it's big so it can be tied around your pirate's head. Hem around the edges.

Challenge

Adapt this outfit to make a costume for a handsome prince.

Glossary

bodkin
a blunt, thick needle to thread elastic or tape

braid
woven thread used as a trim

broderie anglaise
embroidery on white cotton

collage
an arrangement of different materials, such as paper or fabric, glued to a backing

embroidery thread
thick thread used to embroider

fix (ref dyeing)
to stop the colour washing out

fray
to become undone at the edges of the material

haberdashery
equipment used for dress-making, sewing and knitting

hemming fix
adhesive tape that you iron on to hem material

right-sides
the side of the material you want showing when you wear it

rikrak
flat narrow braid woven in zigzag form

symmetrical
a shape that can be divided in half so that one side is a mirror image of the other

template
a piece of material used as a guide for shaping and cutting things that can be used more than once

thimble
a small metal or rubber cap worn on your finger to protect it when sewing

wrong-sides
the side of material you don't want showing when you wear it

Further information

You might find these websites helpful for finding ideas, techniques and materials:

www.childrensscrapstore.co.uk
Information about the Children's scrapstore in Bristol, where scrap materials are recycled and sold for educational art and craft projects. Also includes a list of other scrapstores around the UK.

www.designmuseum.org
The Design Museum, London. Museum of contemporary design.

www.devon.gov.uk/index/learnin g/early_years_and_childcare/dis c_services/toylibr.htm
More scrapstore addresses!

www.en-form.supanet.com/ scrapstores.htm
A directory of UK Scrapstores.

www.fabrics4you.co.uk
Online fabric store – will send samples, too.

www.ftmlondon.org
Fashion and Textile Museum, London. The collection contains items from the 1950s to present day.

www.fun2do.co.uk
Mail order specialists for haberdashery and craft supplies.

www.japanesekimono.com
For lots of information on kimonos, including history and facts.

www.kinderart.com/textiles/ easytiedye.shtml
For more tie-dye ideas.

www.kirbymountain.com/rosenla ke/sarong.html
To find out how to tie a sarong.

www.object.com.au
Object Museum, NSW, Australia. Museum of contemporary design.

www.sherwoodsspirit.com
To look at more wonderful moccasin designs.

www.vam.ac.uk
V&A museum, London. Lots of fashion and textile ideas.

Every effort has been made by the Publisher to ensure that these websites are suitable for children, and contain no inappropriate or offensive material. However, because of the nature of the Internet, it is impossible to guarantee that the contents of these sites will not be altered. We strongly advise that Internet access is supervised by a responsible adult.